The Whale's Journey

Benjamin Tunby

Lerner Publications • Minneapolis

Copyright © 2018 by Lerner Publishing Group, Inc.

All rights reserved. International copyright secured. No part of this book may be reproduced, stored in a retrieval system, or transmitted in any form or by any means—electronic, mechanical, photocopying, recording, or otherwise—without the prior written permission of Lerner Publishing Group, Inc., except for the inclusion of brief quotations in an acknowledged review.

Lerner Publications Company
A division of Lerner Publishing Group, Inc.
241 First Avenue North
Minneapolis, MN 55401 USA

For reading levels and more information, look up this title at www.lernerbooks.com.

Library of Congress Cataloging-in-Publication Data

The Cataloging-in-Publication Data for *The Whale's Journey* is on file at the Library of Congress.
ISBN 978-1-5124-8635-3 (lib. bdg.)
ISBN 978-1-5415-1184-2 (pbk.)
ISBN 978-1-5124-9813-4 (eb pdf)

Manufactured in the United States of America
1-43459-33199-6/27/2017

Table of Contents

Meet the Whale — 4

A Whale Is Born — 8

A Whale Migrates — 11

Whales in Danger — 16

Fun Facts — 20

More Amazing Migrators — 21

Glossary — 22

Further Reading — 23

Index — 24

Meet the Whale

A whale swims slowly through the ocean. Most whales are migrators. They move from one area to another at different times of the year.

Whales are found in every ocean in the world.

Whales have long tails and two fins on their sides. They use them to swim through the water.

Whales are very large creatures. The blue whale can be up to 100 feet (30 m) long.

Humpback whales have two blowholes!

A whale breathes through a blowhole on the back of its head. When this mammal breathes out, a spout of moist, warm air comes out.

Whales eat small fish, krill, shrimp, squid, and octopus. They need lots of energy for their long journey.

Blue whales will eat up to 8,000 pounds (3,630 kg) of food a day!

A Whale Is Born

Splash! A male whale leaps out of the water. This is called breaching. Scientists believe males breach to attract females for mating.

About ten to twelve months after mating, a mother whale gives birth to a baby. A baby whale is called a calf.

Calves can swim right after birth.

Calves drink milk from their mothers. The milk helps calves grow. Soon the calves begin to hunt on their own.

A Whale Migrates

When they are grown up, many whales migrate. The younger whales follow the older whales.

Female sperm whales don't migrate. They stay in the tropics with their young all year.

The gray whale migrates to find food.

A grown-up whale needs to eat a lot of food. Many whales will travel thousands of miles to find food in colder waters. They can find more food there.

Whales build up blubber from all the food they eat. They use this layer of fat for energy during their next migration.

Most whales don't eat while they are migrating.

Humpback Whale Migration

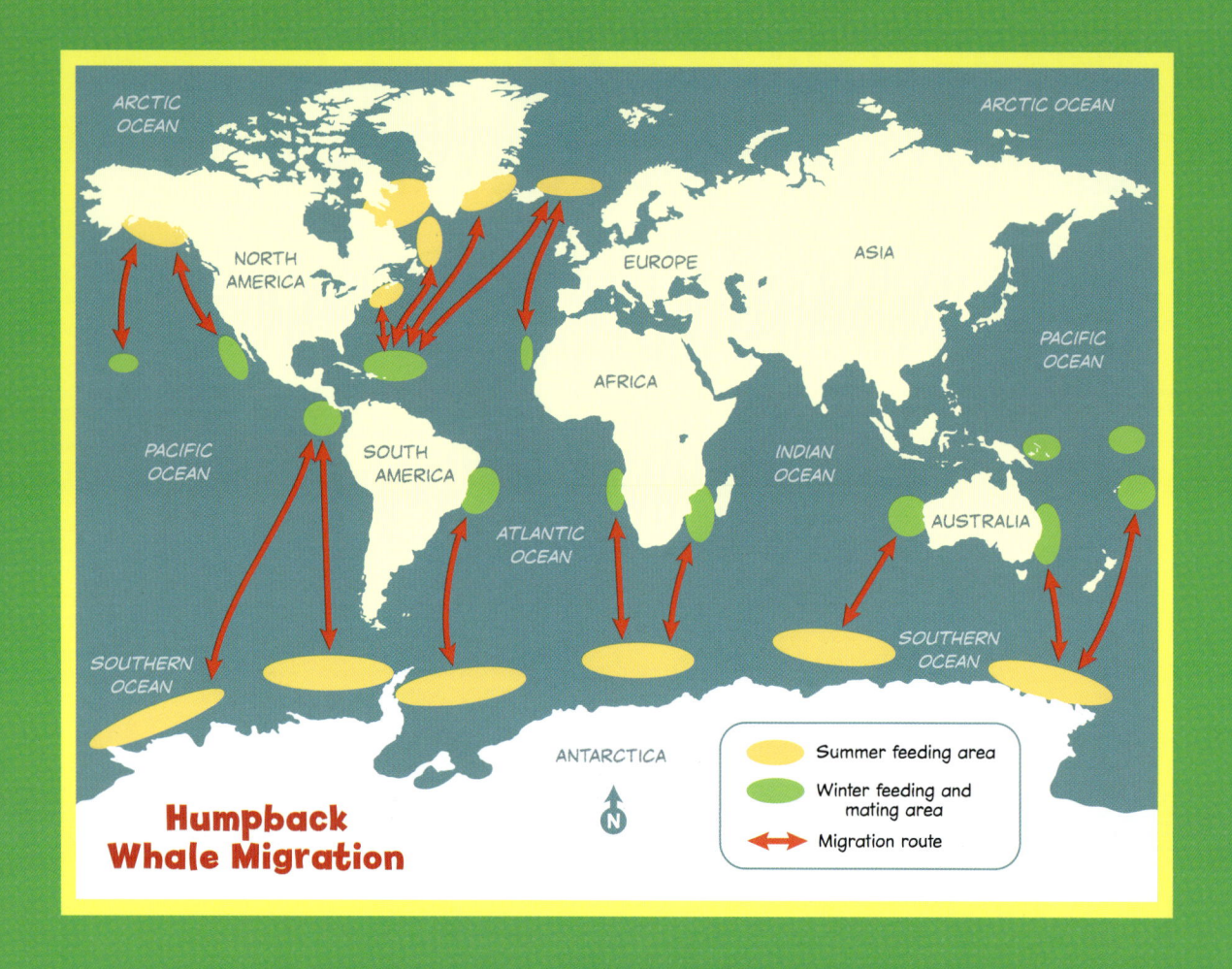

- Summer feeding area
- Winter feeding and mating area
- ↔ Migration route

A grown-up whale finds a mate and has its young. Cold waters are too dangerous for baby whales. A whale must migrate again so it can breed.

A whale will return to the tropics in January or February to have babies. The tropics have warmer waters. The calves stay here until they are ready to migrate.

Whales in Danger

Whales are so large that it's hard for predators to hunt them. Sometimes a group of orcas will attack smaller whales or calves.

Some whales are killed or eaten by predators. Orcas are one of these predators.

Humans are the biggest threat to whales. Sometimes people catch too many fish. Then whales don't have enough to eat. Some people even hunt whales. This is called whaling.

Whales can also get hit by passing boats or caught in fishing nets.

Climate change is another threat to whales. Warming waters can affect how much food whales have. Some whales might not find enough food to survive.

Changes in water temperature greatly affect the health of whales.

Many people are trying to help whales by making laws to protect them. These laws make sure whales will be around for a very long time.

You can help whales by raising money for charities working to protect them.

Fun Facts

- Humpback, bowhead, and sperm are some common types of whales, and they are each different when it comes to migration. Humpback whales migrate, and bowhead whales don't migrate. Male sperm whales migrate, but female sperm whales do not.

- Bowhead whales can live to be two hundred years old. This makes them the longest-living mammals.

- The longest recorded whale migration was completed by a female gray whale. She traveled almost 14,000 miles (22,511 km) in just 172 days!

More Amazing Migrators

- Hammerhead sharks live in tropical waters. They migrate to cooler waters during the summer. They can travel in groups of hundreds.

- A group of stingrays is called a fever. The golden cow-nosed stingrays migrate to their summer feeding grounds. Their fever can include up to ten thousand stingrays.

- Leatherback sea turtles travel thousands of miles. They go to their nesting beach to lay eggs.

Glossary

blowhole: a hole on the top of a whale's head that it breathes through

blubber: saved up fat that can be used for energy

breach: to burst out of the water and splash down

breed: to produce young

climate: the usual pattern of weather in a place over a period of time

mammal: an animal whose females nurse their young with milk

mate: to come together to produce young

migrator: an animal that moves from one area to another at different times of the year

tropics: a warm area of water close to the equator

Further Reading

Boothroyd, Jennifer. *Let's Visit the Ocean*. Minneapolis: Lerner Publications, 2017.

Desmond, Jenni. *The Blue Whale*. New York: Enchanted Lion Books, 2015.

Ducksters: Blue Whale
http://www.ducksters.com/animals/bluewhale.php

Hirsch, Rebecca E. *Humpback Whales: Musical Migrating Mammals*. Minneapolis: Lerner Publications, 2015.

National Geographic Kids: Whale Makes a Surprise Appearance
http://kids.nationalgeographic.com/explore/nature/whale-makes-a-surprise-appearance

WDC: Whale and Dolphin Activities
http://www.wdcs.org/wdcskids/en/interactive.php

Whale-World: Facts about Whales
http://www.whale-world.com/facts-about-whales-for-kids

LERNER SOURCE

Expand learning beyond the printed book. Download free, complementary educational resources for this book from our website, www.lernerresource.com.

Index

blubber, 13

calf, 9–10, 15, 16

fin, 5
food, 7, 12–13

hunt, 10, 16–17

mate, 14
migration, 13–14

whaling, 17

Photo Acknowledgments

The images in this book are used with the permission of: iStock.com/taxofoto, p. 2; Stephen Frink Collection/Alamy Stock Photo, p. 4; Franco Banfi CreativE/WaterFrame/Getty Images, p. 5; iStock.com/evenfh, p. 6; Doc White/Nature Picture Library/Alamy Stock Photo, p. 7; iStock.com/PaulWolf, p. 8; NOAA/NMFS, p. 9; WorldFoto/Alamy Stock Photo, p. 10; iStock.com/ShaneGross, p. 11; G. Lacz/Arco Images GmbH/Alamy Stock Photo, p. 12; Tomas Kotouc/Shutterstock.com, p. 13; © Laura Westlund/Independent Picture Service, p. 14; Hiroya Minakuchi/Minden Pictures/Getty Images, p. 15; Paul Nicklen/National Geographic/Getty Images, p. 16; NOAA, p. 17; Richard Herrmann/Minden Pictures/Getty Images, p. 18; Jeff Greenberg/UIG/Getty Images, p. 19; iStock.com/PaulWolf, p. 22.

Cover: Masa Ushioda/Stephen Frink Collection/Alamy Stock Photo.

Main body text set in Billy Infant regular 28/36. Typeface provided by SparkType.

Bruce County Public Library
1243 MacKenzie Rd.
Port Elgin ON N0H 2C6